BR BLUE
A PERSONAL
REFLECTION

Stephen Owens

AMBERLEY

First published 2019

Amberley Publishing
The Hill, Stroud
Gloucestershire, GL5 4EP

www.amberley-books.com

Copyright © Stephen Owens, 2019

The right of Stephen Owens to be identified as
the Author of this work has been asserted in
accordance with the Copyrights, Designs and
Patents Act 1988.

ISBN 978 1 4456 8990 6 (print)
ISBN 978 1 4456 8991 3 (ebook)

British Library Cataloguing in Publication Data.
A catalogue record for this book is available from
the British Library.

Typesetting by Aura Technology and Software
Services, India. Printed in UK.

Introduction

As I write this introduction, the railway is in the news again. There are questions being asked in Parliament and the Secretary of State for Transport is under pressure. This is all because of the introduction of a new timetable and the ongoing industrial action by one of the trade unions. Some might suggest that this is nothing new – indeed, that it is hardly news at all. And maybe it isn't.

Because of all the problems, people are saying that the railway should be returned to state control. There have been discussions about this previously with some saying openly that the railway should be renationalised. Whether this would solve any of the difficulties is a moot point, but it gives some the opportunity to say how wonderful, or terrible, the railway was in the 1970s and 1980s.

Between the years of 1978 and 1982 I was able to record some of what I saw on the railway. At this time I was as much concerned with photography as I was with the subject matter. I'd been a trainspotter since the mid-1960s, and although the end of steam is where my railway interest is founded, unfortunately I didn't have a camera then. Consequently, I was unable to record what I saw, and thus, to revisit this era, I have to rely on the photographs taken by others, or on my memory.

In those early years, diesel locos simply had numbers to be recorded and saved – very few were actually memorable. Then, in the 1970s, during a period of rationalisation or standardisation, some of the first-generation diesel classes were withdrawn: the Westerns and the Warships, and the Metroviks and the Claytons, for example. Variety, supposedly the 'spice of life', was being abolished.

Ultimately, this resulted in uniformity. What the railway was left with was a limited number of relatively successful loco classes, all decked out in the same British Rail blue livery. I'd got all the loco numbers – well, most of them – and had been to most of the places the railway would take me, all the better to compile a photo collection. Not that I thought anyone would be interested in seeing it... not for fifty years, at least.

To clarify, perhaps I should say that I never worked on the railway, although there may have been periods when I spent more time on the train and at railway stations than I spent at work. A friend did jokingly ask me once if I was a member of ASLEF.

The railway struck me as being both beleaguered and admirable at the same time. I thought it deserved some respect, along with the people who worked on it. What I particularly admired was how the railway operated in adversity – how it made the best of a bad job, having been dealt such a lousy hand. An illustration of this is that, today, a train of three carriages may be provided with two locos. So, how was it that in 1978 one lesser loco was supposed to perform adequately with a train of five, six or seven carriages, or even more?

The railway in the 1970s was essentially the same as it had been in the 1960s, but the steam engines had gone, and so had a lot of the coal traffic that BR was instrumental in perpetuating to fuel the steam engines. The railway was still divided into regions – the Scottish Region, Southern Region and Western Region, for example – and inter-regional services, and their potential, were largely ignored. There were still freight trains, of course: pick-up trains, and shunters stabled in obscure places, and, thankfully, newspapers, mail and parcels still travelled by train. Because of this some stations were a hive of activity, almost twenty-four hours a day, and this may have given the impression that little had changed since the previous decade or the decade before that.

However, there was disquiet in certain circles. The railway, like many of the nationalised industries, was being starved of investment and the deficiencies were beginning to show. It seemed old and tired, despite an advertising campaign declaring that 'This is the age of the train'. True, the West Coast Main Line had been electrified through to Glasgow, but it was glaringly obvious that the additional sections of line which could easily have been done at the same time were not.

Apparently, according to popular legend, the railway was overcrowded and unreliable, the trains were untidy and often dirty, the staff were unhelpful and often rude and the stations were grim: cold and wet during the day, dark and dangerous at night. The cliché 'give a dog a bad name' springs to mind.

For all this, the railway was a masterpiece – a national treasure. It had been constructed in a haphazard way in the previous century, when the railway was seen as the future. Rival entrepreneurs invested huge sums; some lost everything, as did untold numbers of construction workers who lost their lives. I guess, at the time, people in industry were complaining about the limitations of the decaying canal network and were impatient for a faster alternative.

Had the railway been preserved as it was in 1975 or 1965 – or 1955 for that matter – it would be a World Heritage Site today, and people would come for miles to admire its eccentric quirkiness.

The success of rail preservation societies has everything to do with the failure of the railway – specifically, those tasked with being its guardians.

A railway 'fit for the future' is one that people were happy with and proud of in the past; never mind changing things to accommodate an unknown, uncertain future. It would seem that suddenly, the world is run by impatient futurists: people dissatisfied with how things are, and know all about what the future should look like – quite how they know this, I have no idea.

It seems that there has always been confusion about what the railway is actually for. What is the railway supposed to do? Is it a people carrier, for moving the masses, or something else entirely? Ever since the opening of the Channel Tunnel, or, perhaps, the advent of the TGV in France, people have been overly concerned about having ultra-fast trains that can compete with the airlines. In a small country with a high population, such as the UK, this would appear to be totally the wrong way to go. The requirements of the London catchment commuter, or of Birmingham or Greater Manchester, are totally different from the requirements of the occasional long-distance traveller. It would appear that those who use the railway the most are the ones to be inconvenienced the most. If people want to get from London to Edinburgh or Aberdeen in a hurry, then they can fly. If the holidaymaker knows his journey from Preston to London will take two hours forty minutes, then that will usually be okay; if it is ten or twenty minutes quicker, so what? Fast trains can't fly over slower trains on the same track; they can only be delayed by them. Alternatively, the slower trains have to be dispensed with, and the passengers and their revenue lost.

Sometimes, we fail to appreciate that nothing exists in isolation. During the 1970s, there was significant social change taking place in the UK: the Queen's Jubilee, and the Punk Rock revolution are two things well remembered from the period. There was industrial strife, particularly in the state-owned sector, and while in opposition, the government in waiting was hatching a plan to privatise these monopolies. The idea, simplistically, was to sell off the unwanted, uneconomic nationalised industries for a profit, rather than keeping them in public hands and them being a burden to the taxpayer. This idea would not only provide the Exchequer with a profit, it would save them having to raise taxes to support these ailing industries.

It would be some time before the railway would face privatisation, but in the meantime, it would be starved of funds, and run on a shoestring. For all that, and for those who considered this the norm and knew no different, the railway was a joy.

The photographs that follow are intended to illustrate how the railway was rather than how people think it was. They were taken mostly between the years of 1978 and 1982. Before 1978 I had an Instamatic camera, which was better than nothing, but only just. Realising what was happening, with the demise of the hydraulics, I thought I should attempt to capture what I could before it was too late.

Keighley was my home town, and then, later, so was Blackburn. Neither of these places are the centre of anything, and yet there is irony in the fact that the Keighley & Worth Valley Railway was established on my doorstep. Further, Keighley is at the southern end of the Settle–Carlisle, and this may go some way to explaining why I developed an affection for the line.

Blackburn has passenger trains to and from Preston, and all stations to Burnley and Colne, on the truncated East Lancashire Line; there are regular trains to Manchester, via Bolton. The Manchester service was extended through to Clitheroe a few years ago, and the secondary Trans-Pennine route through to Hebden Bridge was upgraded while the Blackpool–Leeds service was improved. Additionally, freight trains and diverted West Coast Main Line services are routed through Blackburn, to join up with the S&C at Hellifield. In the 1970s and 1980s, the winter Sunday diversions were a bonus.

The photos illustrate where I went, if not how I got there. However, there are geographic omissions. Whole swathes of the country appear forgotten: the North East, Cornwall, Kent and Sussex. I've no shots of Norwich and, inexplicably, hardly any of Bristol. Perhaps, at least partially, the reason for this is that whenever I could, I'd go to Scotland, or Leeds and York, or Crewe and Derby.

Difficult to imagine though it may be, when spotting in Keighley in the 1960s seeing the 'Thames Clyde Express' and the 'Waverley' made Carlisle and Scotland seem quite mysterious, and almost exotic, far away destinations. The seeds were sown; I went to Carlisle for the first time in 1968, only a few days after the end of steam. There were still four locos in Kingmoor: Black 5s that had pulled the last steam specials, and No. 44767 was certainly one of them. Peaks had been in charge on the S&C for a while, and these were often Holbeck locos. I do recall being pulled by D17 from Keighley to Lancaster Green Ayre on Easter Monday, 1965. I had to walk to town to catch the train just before 7 a.m. The return was a Black 5.

From Blackburn, the Region 2 Runabout Ticket allowed unlimited travel to Carlisle, and even to Annan. I recall buying my first at Cherry Tree, when it was still manned and had a booking office, and double-headed Class 50s were in charge over Shap. Later, I discovered the Scotland Rover Ticket. What a bargain; buy it one afternoon in Carlisle, and the next morning you could be on the train from Inverness to Wick or Thurso. If I recall, I did my first Scotland Rover in 1978 and my last in 1982. I haven't been to Scotland since, and I dread to think how much the ticket would cost today.

One of the delights of these tickets was the freedom they afforded – the unrestricted access to the network. For all that, I never went to Ayr or Stranraer, and I only went to Berwick once. On the plus side, I had a good hotel in Inverness, a strange one in Glasgow, and I knew that most of the overnight services ran mostly empty, the mail and the newspapers being the most important cargo.

Funnily enough, for most of this period I had a car. This gave me the opportunity to drive to a railhead and leave it on the car park and take the train. It also meant I could drive to places which were difficult to get to on the train: Shirebrook, and Barrow Hill, Knottingly and Immingham, for example.

The car was particularly useful for getting to Settle Junction. In summer I could get there after work in time to capture the last southbound Glasgow–Nottingham train. On other occasions, regardless of the weather or the time of year, I'd drive up to Dent and enjoy going over the hill to Garsdale. After the trains had gone, you really did hope that the car was going to start, realising how remote and precarious the location was.

One thing I enjoyed doing was revisiting the places where we had spent our family summer holidays. Actually, my older brother and I spent most of these holidays at the local railway station, rather than on the beach or sightseeing. We went to Bournemouth in 1966 and then again in 1967. The difference in the two years was shocking: no steam in 1967, and the holiday was a major disappointment. In 1969 we went to Paignton – well, Newton Abbot station, really. Our last family holiday was in 1970, to Tenby. The highlights of this were the visits to Swansea and Cardiff: Westerns, Warships and Hymeks prevailed in these places back then.

Returning to these destinations a decade later proved something – catch it while you can. Where Bournemouth shed had been, across from the long platform to the west of the station, there was a car park. However, on the wall behind the platform, delightfully, the graffiti of loco numbers and names had somehow survived. There was something about this which is difficult to put in to words, perhaps because it is a proof that although time waits for no man, in some places it also stands still.

Newton Abbot didn't appear to have changed in ten years, but the locos that pulled the trains had. Class 50s had been brought in from the North West, and for me they became the 'great pretenders'. They'd had the misfortune to replace our beloved Britannia steam locos in 1967/68, and now they had the double misfortune to replace the Westerns. Was their reputation ever redeemable, good locos though they surely were? The names they were given didn't really help, either, as these were usually hand-me-downs and reminders of more glamorous engines from an earlier era.

At Landore shed, in 1970, we went to ask the foreman if it was okay to go round. He gave us a guide! Later, perhaps 1978 or 1979, I'm pretty sure I asked the same man, and he nodded me in.

On a couple of occasions, I travelled to Swansea on the Central Wales line. I'd discovered that there was a really early or very, very late train from Shrewsbury, at about 3 a.m. I presume this was what was left of a paper or mail train. I went from

Preston to Crewe, Crewe to Shrewsbury, and Shrewsbury to Swansea with a Cross Country DMU doing the honours over Sugar Loaf, in the dark. Regardless, doing the journey felt like an achievement, even if it did leave me feeling like a mail bag.

Going to London was something of a contrast. Although the streets were hardly 'paved with gold', there was an abundance of riches to be found at the railway stations of the capital: one was almost spoilt for choice.

I'd usually arrive there on the train from Preston. If this was the case, my routine was to leave Euston immediately and walk down Euston Road, through St Pancras, to King's Cross. I'd then invariably take the Tube to Liverpool Street and then continue to Waterloo, and finally to Paddington. The only stations where I would spend much time and wait were King's Cross and Paddington. Sometimes I would do this circuit, or an abbreviated version of it, twice in one day. The only London sheds I visited were Old Oak Common and Finsbury Park. I did go to Hither Green once or twice, but not around the shed.

While writing this last sentence, I was reminded that loco sheds were often located in places which had quite enchanting names, largely at odds with their role. However, Nine Elms can certainly be added to the list, and so too can Springs Branch and Rose Grove. Obviously, there are plenty of places which would not make the list, having a name that conjures a totally different image: Farnley, Mirfield and Stourton sound like a firm of solicitors, and Edge Hill a battlefield.

In retrospect, there were advantages in coming from somewhere away from the centre of things. The ordinariness of a small town, with a limited rail service, provided an appreciation of the exceptional. A visit to York could seem chaotic, with constant comings and goings. If I'd lived in a place where Coronations, A4s or Kings had been commonplace, I'm sure I would have become blasé about seeing them and, consequently, lost interest. It was the belief that if we were patient, and prepared to wait optimistically in the rain, then we might be rewarded by seeing something rare or unusual. Occasionally we were rewarded and these events perpetuated our enthusiasm, and, I concede, it didn't always rain.

I never lost interest in the railway, although it may seem like I did. True, I have spent time away, but the railway remains irresistible – a companion to spend time with. However, it should not be taken for granted: it is unpredictable and often likely to do strange things which might cause concern or even offence.

I went to Liverpool recently. I had to be there quite early. Consequently, to ensure that I would arrive in time for my appointment, I had to go on the bus – the ignominy: not for me, but for the railway. Not only was the timetable fluid, Lime Street station was closed. It was being modernised.

I also went through Manchester Victoria recently. The first time I visited was in the mid-1960s. A Jubilee was station pilot, and the walk down to Exchange an adventure. Furthermore, to walk through town to Piccadilly was akin to visiting the future. Although in retrospect I was fortunate to see *Pandora* and the rest of the class on the Sheffield trains, I was none too impressed at the time, and wanted to hurry back to Victoria in case I missed something good.

The facade of Victoria still perpetuates the illusion that you might see something good: the destinations in glass in the wrought-ironwork canopy, and, delightfully, the old Lancashire and Yorkshire map on the white tiled wall. They have retained the wood-panelled booking offices, which is a thoughtful touch, but that's about the sum of it. If you're in a hurry, which the majority of people always seem to be nowadays, these reminders of a stylish past are irrelevant and suitably obscure.

I was not in a hurry, so I had time to notice, and although I had a through ticket to Manchester Airport, rather than take the train or tram, for old times' sake I walked to Piccadilly.

It was a lovely day. Manchester in the sunshine felt distantly Continental; wine bars, pavement cafeterias and the homeless, sleeping in the doorways of businesses that had closed down. I felt ridiculously foreign, carrying my overnight bag. To prove to myself I could communicate, I stopped to talk to someone doing missionary work. He was quite taken aback. We talked about Manchester and how it had changed. We were of a similar age, but he'd spent all his life living in Manchester – imagine that, and you can understand why he was doing missionary work.

I approached Piccadilly station. Once it had been a BR showcase, with fast, efficient electric trains to London. The concourse struck me as being cramped and claustrophobic – definitely a place to leave.

My train to the airport was heading for Crewe on another new bit of line added. Connectivity, they call it, in a mobile, internet-powered world. On the journey we passed Longsight, and I recall that on a Sunday school day trip to Belle Vue Zoo in the 1960s my brother and I stood by the line for a while and saw our first electrics. We didn't stay there long; even then, I found modernity far too troubling. Best get back to the animals, who were protected, and kept in familiar surroundings for a reason.

I never lost interest in the railway. It was the owners that did.

Railway journeys invariably have an inauspicious beginning and, perhaps inevitably, a disappointing end. Obviously, this doesn't only apply to railway journeys, but few other travel options offer such a wide range of destinations.

I once took the train from my local station, Cherry Tree, to Milan. I didn't stop there. I ended up in Brindisi, but not long afterwards I was back where I started. Nothing had changed; I'd only been away two weeks.

Most people who catch the train are not going to the ends of the Earth. They are more likely to be going to work or school, or going to the hospital to fulfil an appointment. Often, when I've had to use the train for an ordinary reason, I've tried to imagine that I'm setting off on some extraordinary journey. I wonder how many commuters fantasise about the same thing – purely as an incentive to get up in a morning. Do they view people with suitcases enviously, or do they see them as a daydream temptation to be ignored?

I've never carried a suitcase, unless it was for someone else. There was a period when I would use a briefcase for my overnight things. I thought it was a good disguise; now, I only carry an overnight bag, and no longer take things with me that I don't need.

There are various books that have done wonders for rail travel: Agatha Christie's *Murder on the Orient Express*, Graham Greene's *Stamboul Train* and John Buchan's *The Thirty-Nine Steps*, for example. Films and television programs, too, have helped to generate or perpetuate a romantic image of rail travel. Other travel books have been much more in keeping with the reality: *The Great Railway Bazaar* by Paul Theroux is a personal favourite.

While travelling around the UK, instead of taking notes of loco numbers, train workings and timings, I'd probably be reading something serious, trying to catch up on all the titles I never read when I should. I was also reading books about beyond the UK – books by Theoux and Naipaul, but others, too, which were often described as 'eccentric travel'. I doubt I ever bought or read a newspaper – a *Melody Maker*, perhaps – although I'd ride on the trains that were delivering them to the remotest places in the UK.

To me, there was nothing more eccentric than spending a week on the train travelling around Scotland. This was also the height of indulgence. Sometimes, in winter, it would seem that the trains were provided especially for me – there were so few passengers on some of them.

I think I first realised in the late 1960s the frustration of collecting numbers. So often we'd see locos that we couldn't get the number of, in sheds or on scrap lines, and then, whenever I got a new loco shed book, I seemed to have far fewer numbers to put in it than I had in my old book.

This was because lots of the engines I'd seen had been withdrawn. Similarly, locos I'd not seen had also been withdrawn, and this meant it was impossible for me to complete the class. I recall being particularly disappointed when *Coeur de Lion* was withdrawn. This was the first Britannia to go. It was a palindrome, No. 70007, and I hadn't seen it. I've had a soft spot for palindromes ever since. History would be repeated years later with the early withdrawal of D322 and D1020, robbing me of the opportunity to complete these two classes. I did go to Swindon to see if by chance *Western Hero* was still there, but it wasn't.

Latterly, I'd simply carry a list of the numbers of the locos that I hadn't seen, but later, when it was down to only a few 31s and 37s, I gave up, and I knew I wouldn't see any of the 33/2s I needed, unless I went south.

Another frustration was the sense that the railway had shrunk and was still shrinking. Lines and stations had been closed. Cherry Tree had once been a junction, but the line to Chorley was closed in the 1960s. In Keighley, we'd lived between two closed lines. The line to Haworth and Oxenhope was preserved by the KWVR, but the other line, the Queenbury route to Halifax and Bradford, was not.

The first time I went to Dumfries, three Class 27 locos were stabled in the western bay. These locos were being used on the lifting trains, which were dismantling the old route to Stranraer. This closure didn't seem to be in any way creditable; indeed, it was as absurd as the closure of the Waverley.

I now consider that I was fortunate to see trains that had travelled the Waverley from Edinburgh to Carlisle. One of my most vivid recollections is of seeing D5310 in green after it had arrived at Carlisle on a freezing cold, dark night in December 1968. The loco appeared to be steaming, like a thoroughbred racehorse after it had run the National.

Equally, I'm disappointed that I missed seeing Glasgow Buchanan Street, and that my recollections of Bradford Forster Square and Exchange have been virtually forgotten.

Railway stations had their own allure. They could be intriguing, with names that conjured notions of grandeur. Many were built by the independent railway companies in the nineteenth century as a statement of intent; the wealth they invested in the stations was surely indicative of the quality of the service they would provide on their trains. Some stations were so well endowed with facilities, why would anyone want to go somewhere else? Some had quite grand hotels nearby. The stations in the railway towns of Crewe, Doncaster, Carlisle and York seemed to play host to a permanent number of dedicated rail enthusiasts; the faces may change, but the number varied little.

I perhaps told people I'd been to Newcastle or Cardiff, or Norwich or Ipswich, but I doubt I ever stepped out of the stations to see what these towns were really like. The first time I went to Lancaster was in 1965. I arrived at Green Ayre and went up to Castle on the old electric units, which were unique. I don't think I set foot in Lancaster until well in to the 1970s.

Lancaster Castle would certainly be one of those stations with a name that 'conjured notions'. Liverpool Lime Street has always been a personal favourite, and does any other station have such a dramatic arrival with forbidding tunnels and immense walls? Bristol Temple Meads, Yeovil Pen Mill, Dundee Tay Bridge, Rannoch Moor, Hull Paragon, Burnley Barracks and Oldham Mumps would all be names requiring an explanation to the curious; at times, English can seem like it's a foreign language.

Some stations were given an additional name because the town was fortunate enough to boast two stations or more. Manchester had Piccadilly, Victoria, Exchange, Deansgate, Oxford Road and Midland. But beyond, and perhaps in quite remote locations, there was Kirkby Stephen West and Kirkby Stephen East, Tyndrum Upper and Tyndrum Lower, and Garsdale was once known as Hawes Junction. Imagine that.

London is awash with railway stations; pity the poor visitor from abroad who has to figure out how to get from London to Exeter:

'You can go from Paddington or Waterloo.'
'No. I want to go from London.'

Once, I heard that a visitor was so confused about getting from London to Oxford that they took a taxi. They then had no money. Similarly, there is the well-known tale of the Asian visitor who asked at Heathrow about getting to Torquay, and was put on a plane to Istanbul, Turkey.

However, London has some special stations, and perhaps some which people will dislike. I should declare here that it is years since I was in London – I've only been once this century, and on that occasion I passed by Victoria without going in.

It was from Victoria that I first left the UK, and later I'd leave the country from Liverpool Street. This was before the building of the Channel Tunnel, but I don't ever recall seeing trains bound for Paris or Brussels at Waterloo. I may have done, but didn't bother to save the memory. I always quite liked Waterloo – maybe because of 'Waterloo Sunset' by the Kinks; a nostalgic song, which now seems terribly dated. I'd walk the bridge to Charing Cross – such a splendid station, with an unrivalled location in the heart of the capital: The Strand and Trafalgar Square; surely, all the trains from the Continent should have arrived here. The idea of sending them in to St Pancras does have its merits, and this station would certainly rank as one of the London favourites. I probably shouldn't say, but I really disliked Euston. This was usually my arrival point, but I couldn't get away fast enough. I'd either take the London Underground or walk down Euston Road to St Pancras and King's Cross. Paddington and Liverpool Street both seemed to be out on a limb, but I liked each of them for their cluttered untidiness. This is an architectural and structural untidiness – nothing to do with the state of the station environment.

There were occasions when I took the train out of or into each of these stations, with one glaring omission: King's Cross. I can offer no explanation as to why this is the case. I did visit Marylebone and Cannon Street, and various suburban stations, but without question I'd spend more time at King's Cross. I'd often stay nearby; there were plenty of hotels and lots of places to eat in the vicinity.

A Class 45/6 Peak at Keighley hauling a northbound coal train on a sunny afternoon in the early 1980s. The photograph was taken from Lawkholme Lane Bridge. As a boy I'd cross this bridge on my way to and from school. Often, in the morning, there would be a Mogul 2-6-0 shunting in the yard; this nearly always seemed to be No. 43030. On the way home from school, spotters would congregate here to see the 15.40 Bradford to Carlisle stopping train, which left Keighley at 16.06. Normally, it was pulled by something worth waiting for. I recall seeing No. 46115 *Scots Guardsman* on it, but always hoped it would be a Britannia; sometimes it was.

A Class 47 to the north of Keighley hauling a Nottingham to Glasgow passenger train on a summer evening in the late 1970s. I'm not certain of the precise location here – Steeton, perhaps, but definitely Airedale.

Class 40 loco No. 40049 at Skipton departing with a Leeds to Carlisle passenger train, while No. 40104 waits for right of way with a freight train, in September 1982. The photo was taken from the bridge we'd go across in the 1960s to walk to the shed.

Class 40 loco No. 40063 hauling a freight train at Skipton in the early 1980s. The photo, taken with a telephoto lens, illustrates the redundant side of the station, and quite forlorn it looks, too.

A Class 40 loco at Skipton hauling a freight train on a Saturday afternoon in the early 1980s. The train is sidelined here and waiting. This is the Heysham Moss to Haverton Hill tanks; I recall seeing a similar train in the late 1960s, being hauled by a Class 37, often with a brake tender. At that time the wasteland in the foreground was occupied by lines, some of which were filled with withdrawn steam locos.

Class 31 No. 31283 at Skipton, looking far from perfect on an overcast afternoon in the early 1980s. This picture is here because of what lies across the tracks, beyond the loco. Skipton shed would have been right there – probably the first shed I went around. There was seldom anything remarkable in the shed – latterly, Standard 4MT 4-6-0 75XXX locos – but occasionally there was. I saw Britannia locos No. 70001 *Lord Hurcombe* with a damaged blink and No. 70040 *Clive of India* inside this shed. The scrap line, which we'd walk past on the way to the shed, was always an interesting if rather melancholic sight.

Class 31 loco No. 31178 enjoying a rest day in the sunshine on the stabling point at Skipton in the late 1970s.

A Class 45/6 Peak at Gargrave, hauling a Nottingham to Glasgow passenger train on a summer evening in the early 1980s.

A Class 47 loco at Hellifield, hauling a northbound diverted WCML passenger train in the early 1980s.

A Class 45/6 Peak loco between Long Preston and Settle Junction hauling a Nottingham to Glasgow passenger train in the early 1980s.

A Class 31 loco at Settle Junction, hauling a Morecambe to Leeds passenger train in the early 1980s. At this time, the service was normally operated by a DMU to facilitate the reverse at Lancaster. The first time I went through this junction was on Easter Monday 1965 on the way to Lancaster Green Ayre, behind Peak D17.

A Class 45 Peak at Settle Junction, hauling a Glasgow to Nottingham passenger train on a sunny day in the early 1980s.

A Class 45 Peak at Settle Junction, hauling a Glasgow to Nottingham passenger train under a dramatic sky in the early 1980s.

A Class 45 Peak loco at Settle Junction, hauling a Glasgow to Nottingham passenger train on a freezing cold day in the early 1980s. As I recall this was around New Year, possibly 1982, and the tundra-like conditions made the drive up quite a challenge. However, I expect this was as nothing compared with the weather this train seems to have experienced on its journey south. There is nothing much worse than freezing fog, but it lends an atmosphere to this picture.

Class 45 Peak loco No. 45027 at Settle, hauling a Glasgow Central to Nottingham passenger train in the late 1970s.

Class 31 loco No. 31180 at Settle, hauling a Carlisle to Leeds passenger train in the summer of 1982. In the background, on the station wall, can be seen the Settle–Carlisle marker arrows: 236 miles to London!

A Class 45/6 Peak loco clears Ribblehead Viaduct as it heads toward Blea Moor while hauling a Nottingham to Glasgow passenger train in the early 1980s. It was marvellous to receive the acknowledgement from the driver here; it seems to make the picture even more special, thanks to him.

Class 25 diesel loco No. 25248 arriving at Carlisle, with a passenger train from Leeds, in the summer of 1982. This was shortly after the through trains from Nottingham to Glasgow had ceased to operate over the Settle-Carlisle. They had been replaced by two trains a day each way between Leeds and Carlisle, which it seemed were hauled by whichever loco was available at the time.

Class 25 loco No. 25042 and Class 40 loco No. 40068 at Carlisle in the summer of 1982. The locos are in the southern bay platforms waiting to depart with their respective passenger trains for Leeds and Newcastle. Both services seemed to be pulled by a random selection of locos; apparently, a couple of days after this photo was taken the Newcastle train was hauled by a Deltic.

Class 40 diesel loco No. 40035 *Apapa* at Carlisle, after arriving with a passenger train from Leeds in September 1982. I'd travelled on this train from Settle, and although *Apapa* – a palindrome – doesn't appear to be in the best condition, we arrived on time. As can be seen, the station lights are on; the nights were drawing in and the sun was setting on the Class 40s.

Class 45 Peak No. 45070 at Carlisle, hauling a passenger train to Leeds and Nottingham in the late 1980s. One of the station clocks is clear to see – it's just after 6 p.m. For years, there was a departure from Carlisle heading south over the S&C at round about this time. I caught it for the first time in 1968. Prior to this, at Keighley we had an 8 p.m. train to Bradford, which had come down from Carlisle. This was often hauled by a Britannia. I travelled on it only once, from Skipton to Keighley, behind No. 70016 *Ariel*. I saw *Oliver Cromwell* on this train, as well as *Alfred the Great*, *Boadicea*, *Clan McGregor* and *Clan McLeod*.

Class 45 Peak No. 45144 *Royal Signals* at Leeds, hauling a passenger train in about 1980.

Class 40 loco No. 40064 at Leeds waiting to depart with a passenger train to Carlisle in 1982. Note the Scottie dog emblem; the loco didn't have this when it arrived in from Carlisle.

Class 31 loco No. 31111 at Leeds, awaiting right of way while hauling a guards van in about 1980. I suspect, although I can't be certain, that this will be heading up to Ribblehead Quarry.

Class 45 Peak No. 45076 at Leeds, probably heading to Neville Hill, in the late 1970s.

Class 47 loco No. 47414 at Leeds, waiting to depart while hauling a passenger train in the late 1970s.

Class 55 Deltic No. 55005 *The Prince of Wales's Own Regiment of Yorkshire* with the stock for a passenger train in the late 1970s. This may have been one of the last occasions I saw a Deltic at Leeds as HSTs were taking over the Leeds to London trains.

Inter-City HST No. 254013 at Leeds in about 1980.

Class 47 locos at Knottingly MPD in the late 1970s. This photo was taken the first time I visited here, which I think was on a Saturday. I only went a couple of times and, as can be seen, at weekends the shed was full of locos that during the week would be busy hauling coal trains.

Class 37 loco No. 37057 at Wath in the sunshine in the late 1970s. This was taken on the only occasion I visited Wath, but it is an excellent reminder, with the loco looking like it was due for a rest.

Class 20 loco No. 20065 at Rotherham hauling a freight train in the late 1970s. This really does look like an image from an earlier era: a train of coal wagons trundling slowly through a station in industrial Yorkshire.

Class 46 Peak loco No. 46014 at York, waiting to depart while hauling a passenger train in about 1980. Meanwhile, Class 55 Deltic No. 55009 arrives hauling a service from London King's Cross.

Class 55 Deltic loco No. 55004 *Queen's Own Highlander* at York, departing with a passenger train to London King's Cross on a gloomy day in the late 1970s.

Class 55 Deltic loco No. 55013 *The Black Watch* at York, departing with a passenger train to London King's Cross on a sunny afternoon in the early 1980s.

Class 55 Deltic loco No. 55021 *Argyll & Sutherland Highlander* at York, hauling a passenger train bathed in glorious sunshine in the early 1980s.

Class 55 Deltic loco No. 55008 *The Green Howards* reversing onto a northbound passenger train in the early 1980s. I think the train is a West Country to Newcastle service, which had a scheduled loco change at York.

Class 31 loco No. 31142 heading through York light engine in the late 1970s. The loco is yet to receive its domino dots and, amusingly, the mini-ploughs appear to have the fixing instructions writ large for all to see.

Class 47 loco No. 47270 at York, all steamed up and hauling a passenger train on a freezing cold day in the early 1980s. The train is in the centre roads and if I recall correctly the carriages were empty, but wherever it was going and whatever it was doing, to see so much steam at York again was quite a sight.

Class 45 Peak No. 45014 *The Cheshire Regiment* bathed in delicious light at York in the late 1970s.

Class 40 loco No. 40192 at York in the late 1970s. I always thought of this line as death row. Locos seen here were often in need of attention, and if the repair was not economically viable, the loco would be withdrawn. I have a vivid memory of seeing A1s *Sir Walter Scott* and *Sir Vincent Raven* hereabouts in the mid-1960s.

Class 08 shunter No. 08197 at York in the early 1980s. At the time I was probably a little annoyed that this was blocking a potential shot of the Class 40 behind, and on such a perfect day, too. Still, I took the photo, and I'm glad I did.

Class 20 loco No. 20144 at Scunthorpe in the sunshine in the late 1970s. The brilliant clouds in the background help make the picture special.

Class 31 loco No. 31144 in the late 1970s. I'm uncertain of the location, but didn't think this a sufficient reason for excluding the photo from this selection. The loco is allocated to Immingham, and it may well be there or, possibly more likely, at Frodingham.

Class 55 Deltic No. 55012 *Crepello* departing from Doncaster with a southbound passenger train in about 1980.

Class 55 Deltic No. 55022 *Royal Scots Grey* departing from Doncaster with a southbound passenger train in about 1980. It seemed on some occasions that all you had to do was stand and wait, and if the sun was shining you'd be compensated for all your previous disappointments.

Class 56 diesel loco No. 56076 stabled at Barrow Hill in the early 1980s. This was an unusual location for me to visit. I drove there one Sunday and also visited Shirebrook and Westhouses. Each of these sheds was predominantly a freight loco depot, and it seemed that on a Sunday they were virtually deserted.

Class 20 diesel loco No. 20059 stabled at Barrow Hill in the early 1980s.

Class 20 loco No. 20183 at Westhouses in the early 1980s. I say on page 77 that Reddish was a little unusual. Westhouses was even more unusual. Again my visit was on a Sunday, and the place really was deserted. It also seemed to be in the middle of nowhere, although I'm sure it can't be.

Class 31 loco No. 31255 at King's Lynn after arriving with a passenger train in the late 1970s.

Class 37 loco No. 37114, also at King's Lynn after arriving with a passenger train in the late 1970s.

Class 31 diesel locos, with No. 31229 leading, at Birmingham New Street while hauling a passenger train from Norwich in the late 1970s. The photo will have been taken on a summer Saturday. When I'd taken this train from Nuneaton to Norwich sometime earlier it was hauled by a pair of 25s.

Class 86 electric loco No. 86012 awaiting duty at Birmingham New Street in the late 1970s. There were occasions when New Street seemed to have lots going on, because trains often had a loco change and this would maintain a degree of interest.

Class 20 diesel locos, with No. 20071 leading, at Derby while hauling a freight train in the early 1980s. No. 20071 still has its tablet catcher recess from the time when it was allocated to Scotland, and here all the discs are open. I don't know Derby well enough to say that this is running wrong line, but trains on this platform usually headed the other way.

Class 47 loco No. 47077 *North Star* at Derby, hauling a parcels train in the late 1970s. Of interest are the odd location for this loco, the steam from the boiler and the unusual white discs on the front. Additionally, it appears the loco may have once had an old shed plate, under the Brush manufacturer plate.

A Class 40 loco passing through Crewe while hauling a coal train in the early 1980s. The 40 is named; I wondered if it was perhaps No. 20 *Franconia*. Overhead wires and catenary are not the most beautiful paraphernalia to help bring out the best in a photo, but here they seem to work just fine, with the lines going here-and-there under a clear blue sky.

A Class 24 loco hauling a coal train at Crewe in the late 1970s. I am delighted to have this one decent photo of a 24 doing what 24s did. There was a time when they were commonplace, especially around Crewe, Stoke, Manchester and in Scotland. Then, mysteriously, they were suddenly gone. I think No. 81 was the last one.

Class 33 loco No. 33013 at Crewe in the early 1980s. Here, the loco is being released from the bay platform, the carriage stock having been removed. This illustrates one of the main reasons why DMUs are so popular with train operators: they eliminate shunting.

A Class 33 loco departing from Crewe while hauling a passenger train to Cardiff in the early 1980s. The Class 33s took over the Crewe–Cardiff service from the Class 25s. Up until then they were seldom seen in this part of the world.

Class 82 electric loco No. 82004 at Crewe, hauling a passenger train in the early 1980s. This is an example of one of the smaller classes of electric. The 82s had a plain, simple design, and they were quite handsome in their own functional way, even with the modified front.

A Class 33 loco at Wem, hauling a Crewe to Cardiff passenger train in the early 1980s. I was travelling on this train, but as the crossing was closed and the signal down I thought I had the opportunity to take the photo. I notice I didn't close the door properly, just in case.

Class 120 Cross Country DMUs at Shrewsbury in the south bay platforms in the late 1970s. The unit on the right is fitted with a headlight for working the central Wales route to Swansea.

A Class 47 at Craven Arms hauling a southbound freight train in the late 1970s. For me, this was quite a remote, far away location. This was possibly because the junction to the south of the station, although appearing distinctly ordinary, provided access to the intriguing, almost mysterious line to Swansea.

Class 25 loco No. 25042 at Hereford, hauling a Crewe to Cardiff passenger train in the early 1980s.

Class 25 loco No. 25224 at Cardiff after arriving with a passenger train from Crewe in the late 1970s.

Class 33 loco No. 33018 heads off to the carriage sidings after arriving at Cardiff with a passenger train in the early 1980s. It appears two freight trains were passing through on the centre roads – I like the guard and the guard's van; and a DMU may be about to head off to one of the valleys.

A Class 37 loco hauling an early evening passenger train at Cardiff in the early 1980s.

Class 31 loco No. 31401 hauling a parcels train at Bristol in the late 1970s. Seeing that I went to Bristol quite often, it is somewhat baffling that I have so few photos taken here. I recall seeing Westerns and Warships, and *Falcon* at Temple Meads. Be that as it may, this humble 31, in its striking condition, is my only image taken at Bristol in this collection.

Class 33 loco No. 33008 at Exeter waiting to depart with a passenger train to London Waterloo in the late 1970s. Exeter was a popular location because of the variety of locos which would be seen on the inter-regional trains. The first time I visited here this train would most likely have been hauled by a Class 42 Warship.

Class 50 loco No. 50023 *Howe* at Exeter, hauling a westbound passenger train in the early 1980s. Although I preferred the Class 52 Westerns, which the Class 50s succeeded, they were popular in the West Country. Unfortunately, I'd seen them when they were initially introduced in the North West, on the WCML, taking over from the more illustrious steam locos. They were named when they went south, but whether this made them any more memorable I'm unable to say.

A Class 45/6 Peak loco and a Class 47 at Newton Abbot, hauling passenger trains in different directions in the late 1970s. This is the north end of the station, and it is fitting that the Peak should be heading north. I spent much of my 1969 summer holiday on this station, when Westerns and Warships dominated.

Class 45 Peak loco No. 45038 hauling a southbound passenger train at Newton Abbot in the late 1970s.

Class 50 loco No. 50019 *Ramilles* hauling a southbound passenger train at Newton Abbot in the late 1970s.

Class 47 loco No. 47484 *Isambard Kingdom Brunel* at Totnes while hauling a passenger train in the late 1970s. I think I only visited Totnes once, but I saw this loco quite a few times in various locations.

A Class 33/1 loco arriving at Weymouth with a passenger train consisting of an EMU in the late 1970s. This is the only photo I have taken at Weymouth, on the only occasion I have ever been. I don't recall going beyond the confines of the station.

Class 33 loco No. 33006 standing to the west of the station at Bournemouth with empty stock in the late 1970s. Behind the loco, where the cars are parked, were the lines to the loco shed. Behind me and to the left, on the station wall, graffiti was still visible when I took this photo to inform those interested of the numbers and names of some of the steam locos that had once been spotted on shed. We had two summer holidays at Bournemouth in 1966 and 1967. Most of those holidays were spent on this station, although, disappointingly, steam had gone by 1967.

Class 73 electro-diesel No. 73101 at Bournemouth in the late 1970s. These hybrid locos were seldom seen anywhere but on the Southern Region, until recently.

Class 33 locos leaving Basingstoke while hauling a London Waterloo to Exeter passenger train in the early 1980s. The lead loco appears to be freshly outshopped after overhaul and is probably on a running-in trial.

Class 33 loco No. 33110 at Basingstoke while hauling a passenger train in the early 1980s.

Class 50 loco No. 50022 *Anson* hauling a passenger train at Basingstoke in the early 1980s.

Class 33 loco No. 33019 at Woking while hauling a London Waterloo to Exeter passenger train in the early 1980s.

Class 33 loco No. 33202 at Hither Green, hauling a freight train in the late 1970s. I didn't see all of these 33/2s, but I was happy to capture two photos of one of them on a cold autumn day in south London.

Class 33 loco No. 33202 departing Hither Green while hauling a freight train in the late 1970s. It is being passed by a Hastings line Class 202 DEMU.

Class 33 loco No. 33007 at London Waterloo, waiting to depart with a train to Exeter in the late 1970s. Meanwhile, an EMU approaches.

Class 33/1 loco No. 33114 at London Waterloo in the late 1970s. It appears the loco has delivered some empty stock for a passenger train, but I have little recollection of the occasion, though I particularly like the photo.

Class 50 loco No. 50027 *Lion* arriving at London Paddington while hauling a passenger train in the early 1980s.

Class 45 Peak loco No. 45145 at London St Pancras in the late 1970s.

A Class 47 loco at London King's Cross with a parcels train in the early 1980s. The photo was taken at 1.40 a.m. The train is being loaded with parcels, mail and papers prior to its departure north; it steams gently, patiently waiting, under the impressive and stylish roof.

Class 55 Deltic locos Nos 12 *Crepello* and 16 *Gordon Highlander* at the buffers early one morning in the late 1970s. No. 16 was one of my first two Deltics. I saw it and No. 9 at York one Sunday afternoon in about 1964; they were both green, and one of the two, probably No. 16, hadn't yet acquired its name. Not sure if 'Scot' No. 46106 with the same name was still running – maybe it was.

Four HST InterCity 125 trains at London King's Cross in the early 1980s. At this time, these trains were new and represented a modern future for the passenger rail network. I never took many photos of them, but this stark mono certainly works well. One of the trains is much less obvious than the other three.

Class 37 loco No. 37021 at London Liverpool Street in the late 1970s.

Class 47 loco arriving in Blackburn with a winter Sunday diverted West Coast Main Line service, probably in late 1981. The train has been routed over the Settle–Carlisle to Hellifield and then to Blackburn and Preston. At Preston the train would resume its journey south, the Class 47 being replaced by an electric loco. After 4 p.m. the WCML reopened and things in Blackburn returned to normal. The last diverted train of the day was the southbound Red Bank empty vans, which was through Blackburn at about 4 p.m.

A pair of Class 37 locos passing through Blackburn with the Preston to Immingham bitumen train in 1982. This service still operates today, although the scene recorded here has changed immeasurably.

Class 40 loco No. 40025 *Lusitania* at Blackburn on the avoiding line at the head of a freight train on a lovely summer evening, probably in 1982. Also in the shot are stabled DMUs and the old Lancashire & Yorkshire goods shed, as well as the green hills of Lancashire. The old shed has since been demolished and is now a car park, with retail outlets nearby. Recently, I was told that when it was demolished they found that there was still a crane inside.

Class 40 loco No. 40174 awaits the right of way at Blackburn while hauling a freight train in the early 1980s. A Class 47 departs while also hauling a freight train. I'm not sure where either of these are going, but it is likely the Class 40 is heading north over the S&C whereas the Class 47 is probably heading east over Copy Pit.

Class 47 loco No. 47076 *City of Truro* at Blackburn hauling a freight train in the early 1980s. This was an unusual loco to see here; it is a long way from home, being allocated to Cardiff at the time. In the background is part of the building that was the crew signing-on point. Before the changes to the station evident in the shot, this was the main westbound platform.

Class 37 loco No. 37133 at rest in Blackburn station in the summer of 1982. At this time, Blackburn was a signing-on point and the stabling point would invariably have a small collection of Class 25s and 40s. The 37s started to appear more often as the 40s became depleted.

Class 25 loco No. 25156 at Blackburn heading west with a permanent way train. The shot was taken on a summer evening in about 1982, and another Class 25 can be seen on the stabling point. The train is probably heading from the quarry at Ribblehead to Bamber Bridge Sidings.

Class 40 locos Nos 40117, 40183 and 40192 on the stabling point at Blackburn on a summer evening in 1978.

Class 40 locos Nos 40183 and 40117 on the stabling point at Blackburn on a summer evening in 1978.

Class 40 diesel locos, with No. 400064 on the left, on the stabling point at Blackburn on a summer evening in 1982. No. 40064 had for a long time been a Haymarket loco before being transferred south; its battle scars are clearly visible. The two lines of the stabling point once had platforms on either side, and trains to Chorley and beyond would depart from the bay.

Class 25 loco No. 25070 hauling a maintenance train at Blackburn on a summer evening in the late 1970s.

A mixed formation DMU leaving Blackburn for Manchester Victoria is seen passing the site of the old Lower Darwen shed in the autumn of 1982. The floodlights of Ewood Park, home of Blackburn Rovers, can be seen in the background.

A Class 104 DMU at Cherry Tree with a Colne to Preston service on a wintry day in the early 1980s. Imagine arriving here on a day like this, having travelled from the other end of the Earth. I have a recollection that this photo was taken on a Sunday. The arriving passengers are carefully making their way up the untreated, treacherous slope, and the children on the bridge are possibly about to throw snowballs. This railway station, like any other, can be a departure point to somewhere far away, or a welcome home.

Class 40 loco No. 40125 at Cherry Tree, hauling a westbound freight train into the sun in the late 1970s. This loco was the first of the class with a split headcode; the four warning flashes on the nose help identify the loco as No. 40125.

Class 40 loco No. 40076 trundles through Cherry Tree station on its way toward Blackburn with a freight train in 1982. I suppose a few years earlier this train would have been pulled by a Stanier 8F 2-8-0 steam loco. The black and white reproduction certainly gives the picture a stirring atmosphere redolent of the past. All my early railway memories are filed away in black and white, and all those days were grey and rainy. This is obviously not the case, as this collection of pictures illustrates, but this one is most certainly a reminder of those earlier days. There are three bridges visible in the shot: the first carries Green Lane, from which there is access to the station; the second carries the A674, known here as Preston Old Road; the third, in the far distance, is a footbridge only, which links a housing estate with Pleasington Fields. Only the first bridge is an L&Y original.

Class 37 locos Nos 37221 and 37201 at Cherry Tree hauling the empty bitumen tanks from Preston to Immingham in the late summer of 1982.

Class 40 loco No. 40012 *Aureol* running wrong line at Cherry Tree with a freight train on a summer day in the late 1970s. I can't recall the reason for the wrong-line working, but something must have happened on the line: the loco's cab door is open and there is a Hi-Viz jacket visible at the rear of the train. I think it was stopped here, and I had to leave before it did, but this may be an unreliable recollection.

Class 20 locos, with No. 20174 leading, at Cherry Tree, to the west of Blackburn, hauling a freight train on an atmospheric summer morning in the early 1980s. This was the only occasion that I saw Class 20s here. There appears to be a few extra personnel in the cabs of the locos; there was possibly crew training underway.

Class 25 locos Nos 25130 and 25145 at Cherry Tree, hauling a westbound cement train toward Preston, in the early 1980s.

Class 40 loco No. 40009 at Cherry Tree while hauling a westbound freight train into the setting sun on a glorious early evening in the early 1980s. This was one of the first photographs I took in this location using a 135 mm telephoto lens. Actually, it might be the very first, and perhaps it is an example of beginner's luck, but try as I might I never took another shot here that was better than this.

Class 40 loco No. 40141 hauling a late afternoon westbound freight train at Cherry Tree in the early 1980s.

Class 47 loco No. 47570 at Cherry Tree, hauling a diverted WCML passenger train toward Preston in the early 1980s. It is perhaps a little unusual that the buffet is directly behind the loco on this train. This was possibly to facilitate removal at Preston.

A Class 47 loco nears Cherry Tree while hauling a diverted WCML passenger train toward Blackburn in the autumn of 1982.

Class 25 loco No. 25062 nears Cherry Tree while hauling a short permanent way train toward Blackburn on a bright blue morning in the summer of 1982.

Class 40 locos, with No. 40139 leading, are seen between Pleasington and Cherry Tree while hauling a freight train toward Blackburn on a summer evening in the early 1980s. It was quite unusual to see Class 40s double-headed; I'm not sure if it was because of a loco failure, or if it was a balance working.

A Class 40 loco between Pleasington and Cherry Tree, hauling a freight train toward Blackburn in the early 1980s. The hill in the distance is at Hoghton, Preston, which makes quite a steep incline for the railway: Hoghton Bank. This generates lots of noise from trains travelling in either direction. In this shot the train will be coasting – trundling through green pastures and a field of buttercups, before heading down the hill into Blackburn.

A Class 108 DMU nears Cherry Tree, heading toward Blackburn, on a Preston to Colne service in the summer of 1982. I've captioned this as Preston–Colne, but the service may well have operated through from Blackpool South; it often did, but not always. The western end of the service carried far more passengers than the East Lancashire section did. Once the line from Colne to Skipton had been closed, it seemed the towns of Nelson and Colne became forgotten.

A Class 105 Cravens DMU nears Cherry Tree, heading toward Blackburn, on a Preston to Colne service in October 1982. There is something distinctly ordinary about this scene, and it is that which sets it apart. These units were once commonplace on this line, but by this time they were being replaced by others from the same era. However, this was only temporary, and Pacers and Sprinters have dominated the service for the last twenty years and more. Remarkably, I have the unit numbers: M50757 leading M50815.

A Class 101 DMU nears Cherry Tree on a Blackpool North to Leeds service on a wintry day in the early 1980s. At this time, there was only one train a day operating this through service on this line. This return working passed Cherry Tree between 2 and 3 p.m. Today, this service has been expanded and much improved, with hourly trains, some of which run through to York.

A Class 40 loco hauling a freight train between Cherry Tree and Pleasington in the late 1970s. In the background on the right can be seen the embankment which carried the line from Cherry Tree Junction to Chorley.

Another Class 40 loco seen hauling a freight train between Cherry Tree and Pleasington on a summer evening in the late 1970s.

Class 45 Peak loco No. 45006 *Honourable Artillery Company* at Hoghton while hauling the Blackpool to Sheffield summer Saturday-only passenger train in the early 1980s.

Class 47 loco No. 47501 at Preston, hauling electric loco No. 87001 *Royal Scot* and its passenger train in the late 1970s. The 47 would be detached at Preston and the 87 would take the train north.

Class 40 loco No. 40020 *Franconia* at Preston, hauling two other members of the class and an unidentified electric loco in the early 1980s.

Class 82 electric loco No. 82005, hauling a northbound passenger train at Preston in the late 1970s.

Class 83 electric loco No. 83011, hauling a freight train at Preston on a summer evening in the late 1970s.

Class 87 electric loco No. 87013 *John of Gaunt* hauling a northbound passenger train at Preston in the early 1980s. This Class 87 carried the name of the first Britannia steam loco I saw, which was numbered 70012. I appreciated and thought it interesting that the railway handed down names from loco to loco in this way, in a chain of succession. It provided a historical context and gave a sense of continuity – important to both the railway workers and the passengers.

Class 87 electric loco No. 87026 *Redgauntlet* hauling a southbound passenger train at Preston in the late 1970s.

A Class 40 loco at Preston being either detached or attached to Class 87 electric loco No. 87035 *Robert Burns*, which is hauling a northbound passenger train in the late 1970s. If I recall correctly, the Class 40 was being attached, but I can't be certain.

A Class 40 loco arriving with a passenger train at Preston, while Class 86 loco No. 86248 waits to depart with a northbound service in the late 1970s.

A Class 45 Peak, as well as a Class 25, 40 and 47, on the stabling point at Preston in the late 1970s. It was quite rare to see a Peak at Preston at this time, whereas the other locos seen here would be regulars.

Class 40 loco No. 40155 awaiting duty at Blackpool North in 1982. Actually, this is my only photo at Blackpool. I can offer no explanation as to why this should be, but the semaphores and the signal box make the image rather special.

Class 40 loco No. 40091 hauling a northbound freight train at Lancaster in the summer of 1982.

Class 47 loco No. 47335 at Hest Bank, hauling a passenger train in the summer of 1982. This is where the West Coast Main Line brushes the coast, so to speak. Here we see a Brush 47/3, with no train heating, hauling a passenger train. Still, it is summer and I guess the passengers won't mind. In the 1960s, as the end of steam loomed, Hest Bank was a popular place with rail fans, being so close to Carnforth, which had become a steam haven. I was fortunate to spend a week in a caravan here in about 1966, which was wonderful. Back then there were camping coaches parked just to the south of the station, which was open; I recall taking the train to Carnforth behind Britannia No. 70025 *Western Star*.

A Class 40 loco hauling a southbound parcels train at Leyland on a summer evening in 1982.

Class 47 loco No. 47556 hauling a northbound passenger train at Leyland on a summer evening in 1982. The train is possibly from Manchester or Liverpool and would have a change of loco at Preston if it was heading for Scotland.

Class 25 loco No. 25032 at Wigan Springs Branch MPD in the early 1980s.

Class 47 loco No. 47562, also at Wigan Springs Branch MPD in the early 1980s.

A Class 47 loco departing Manchester Piccadilly in the early 1980s. The photograph is complemented by the inclusion of the two approaching Class 304 EMUs, the 08 shunter and the Class 83 loco in the distance.

Class 31 loco No. 31180 at Manchester Victoria on pilot duty, perhaps, in the early 1980s. The first time I was on Victoria was in the mid-1960s, and a Jubilee steam loco was standing in the same place and acting as pilot for the day. One of the loco's duties was to bank heavy freight trains up the hill to Miles Platting.

Class 40 loco No. 40015 *Aquitania* heads through the centre roads of Manchester Victoria while hauling a freight train in the summer of 1982. No. 40181 is acting as pilot, and a Class 104 DMU is waiting to depart with a Southport service. Once this was a typical scene at Manchester Victoria, although seeing the station today this may be somewhat difficult to believe.

Class 40 loco No. 40034 *Accra* at Manchester Victoria, hauling a passenger train in the late 1970s.

Class 45 Peak loco No. 45006 *Honourable Artillery Company* at Manchester Victoria, hauling a passenger train in the late 1970s.

Class 76 electric loco No. 76029 at Reddish in the late 1970s. Gone but not forgotten, these popular locos ran on the unique line from Manchester through Penistone to Sheffield. I visited Reddish three or four times, nearly always on a Sunday afternoon. It was slightly unusual and, invariably, deserted.

Class 40 locos Nos 40192 and 40096 at Buxton in the summer of 1982.

Class 40 loco No. 40025 *Lusitania* at Liverpool Lime Street in the early 1980s. Such a fine loco, and one with a famous name, in the safe harbour of one of my favourite railway stations. We go back a long time, and although I seem to have visited Manchester more often, I still have occasion to visit Lime Street: down the hill, through the tunnels, with the mighty walls on either side of the tracks – such drama.

Class 40 loco No. 40134 at Liverpool Lime Street in the late 1970s. Here, the loco is reversing on to carriages to haul a passenger train which I'm pretty sure I travelled on to Preston.

Class 26 loco No. 26036 at Dumfries, hauling a Glasgow Central to Carlisle passenger train in the summer of 1982. To some extent, almost by default, this service benefited after the loss of the Glasgow to Nottingham service, which ran via the G&SWR and the S&C. It provided an opportunity to see smaller locos hauling short passenger trains.

Class 20 loco No. 20175 at Glasgow Central, where it was working as station pilot, in the early 1980s.

Class 27 loco No. 27004 waiting to depart Glasgow Queen Street as a Class 27-powered push-pull service clears the station bound for Edinburgh on a wet day in the late 1970s.

Class 27 loco No. 27111 hauling a passenger train at Glasgow Queen Street in the late 1970s.

Class 37 loco No. 37012 waiting to depart Glasgow Queen Street with a passenger train in 1982.

Class 37 loco No. 37192 steams gently at the buffers at Glasgow Queen Street with the stock for the overnight service to Inverness in the early 1980s.

Class 47 loco No. 47210 waiting to depart Glasgow Queen Street with a passenger train in the early 1980s. Meanwhile, a Class 47/7 departs with a passenger train to Edinburgh.

Class 47/7 loco No. 47712 *Lady Diana Spencer* at Glasgow Queen Street while hauling a passenger train to Edinburgh in the early 1980s.

Class 27 loco No. 27005 at Eastfield, Glasgow, in the late 1970s. The loco has yet to receive its domino dots in the headcode and the number looks unusually high. For some strange reason, this shot suggests that 27s had something in common with the looks of the Hawker Hurricane.

Class 27 loco No. 27012 at Eastfield, Glasgow, in the late 1970s. There never were such times: Eastfield with 27s basking in the sunshine. This shot of No. 27012 is a personal favourite, with its tablet catcher recess clearly displayed.

Class 27 loco No. 27024 at Motherwell MPD in about 1980. This Class 27 is one of the lesser spotted freight-only locos. There were five of them, and I probably saw this one more times than I saw all the others put together.

Class 25 loco No. 25237 at Edinburgh Waverley in the late 1970s. The loco has just been detached from a parcels train, under cover, on a sunny day. I never took many pictures here, preferring the photo opportunities at Haymarket.

Class 26 loco No. 26027 departing Haymarket in charge of an Edinburgh to Dundee passenger train in the early 1980s. The detail differences of the 26/1 are clearly illustrated in the picture. The loco has sliding windows, round buffers, square steps and the brake cable is in a higher position. It has been fitted with mini-ploughs and the horn cover has had an additional protective shield fitted.

Class 26 loco No. 26030 emerges from the tunnel to arrive at Haymarket with an Edinburgh to Dundee passenger train in the early 1980s.

Class 27 loco No. 27108 at Haymarket while pushing a Glasgow Queen Street to Edinburgh passenger train in the late 1970s. While it lasted the push-pull service was good entertainment, and a forerunner of things to come.

Class 25 loco No. 25075 at Haymarket MPD on a sunny day in the late 1970s.

Class 26 loco No. 26003 at Haymarket MPD on a sunny day in the late 1970s. The photo clearly illustrates some of the detail differences between the Class 26/0 (the first twenty) and the 26/1s. The loco here has drop windows, oval buffers and tapered steps, and the brake cable is in line with the buffers; this made it problematic fitting these locos with the mini-ploughs that the later members of the class nearly all had. No. 26003 also had headboard brackets, front centre, as opposed to lamp brackets above the buffers. D5300, later renumbered 26007, was unique, having four brackets. This loco was allocated to HA for most of its working life.

Class 40 loco No. 40148, also at Haymarket MPD on a sunny day in the late 1970s.

Class 55 Deltic No. 55022 *Royal Scots Grey* at Haymarket MPD in the late 1970s.

Class 27 loco No. 27104 and a Class 26, possibly No. 26022, are seen at Stirling while hauling a Dundee to Glasgow Queen Street passenger train in the late 1970s. No. 27104 appears freshly outshopped from overhaul and will be on a running-in trial.

Piloting a Class 26, Class 40 loco No. 40083 is hauling a southbound freight train at Stirling in the late 1970s.

Class 26 loco No. 26025, in the southern bay at Perth, is hauling a passenger train in the early 1980s.

Class 47 loco No. 47210 and Class 26 loco No. 26044 in the bay platforms at Dundee Tay Bridge, waiting to depart with their respective passenger trains to Glasgow Queen Street and Edinburgh Waverley in the early 1980s.

Class 26 loco No. 26014 at Montrose in about 1980. I took this photo from the train I was on while heading north to Aberdeen. The Class 26 was probably being held here to allow us to pass. Perhaps strangely, I have never set foot in Montrose, although I've passed through on the train.

Class 40 loco No. 40164 leaving Aberdeen and heading south to either Edinburgh or Glasgow. At this time the loco would be allocated to Haymarket.

Class 27 loco No. 27106 departing Keith with an Aberdeen to Inverness passenger train in the early 1980s. The first time I went on this route the trains were operated by Class 120 DMUs. The introduction of the loco-hauled trains was a bonus, allowing for an extended formation, usually of five carriages. At this time there was an increased availability of locos because the Class 27s were being displaced by 47/7s on the Glasgow–Edinburgh service.

Class 26 loco No. 26015 at Inverness MPD in the early 1980s. This loco was unique as it was the only 26/0 to be fitted with the double headlights. The others were Nos 22, 30, 32, 35, 38, 39, 41, 42, 43, 45 and 46.

Class 26 loco No. 26041 reversing into Inverness station with a passenger train from Wick and Thurso in the late 1970s. The train will have bypassed the station on the avoiding line, probably because the northern departure platforms would be occupied. This was a frequent occurrence early in the morning, and probably a source of annoyance to passengers and crew alike.

Class 26 loco No. 26042 passing the shed at Inverness while hauling empty stock in the early 1980s. The carriages will be reversed into the station to form a train to Kyle of Lochalsh.

Class 26 loco No. 26042 arriving at Inverness while hauling the early morning passenger train from Kyle of Lochalsh in the early 1980s.

Class 26 loco No. 26034 arriving at Dingwall while hauling an Inverness to Wick and Thurso passenger train in about 1980. The low winter sun helped produce an atmospheric photo, with the semaphore and the signal box and the smoke from the chimneys of the houses on the right.

Class 26 loco No. 26018 arrives at Brora, from Inverness, with a passenger train for Wick and Thurso in the late 1970s. I was on the southbound service, but knowing this was the crew change station, I was prepared for the photo opportunity. It provides an interesting view of platform life too, with the Royal Mail van in the background, the lady with the children and the crew, who are clearly happy to be reunited with No. 26018 to take it back north.

Class 26 loco No. 26035 at Thurso after arriving with a passenger train from Inverness on a wet day in the late 1970s. It's impossible to beat this photo for atmosphere. It appears a perfect place to end or begin a journey: fancy the walk to Scrabster to take the sailing to Stromness?